21st Century Skills Library

CITIZENS AND THEIR GOVERNMENTS

ELECTING LEADERS

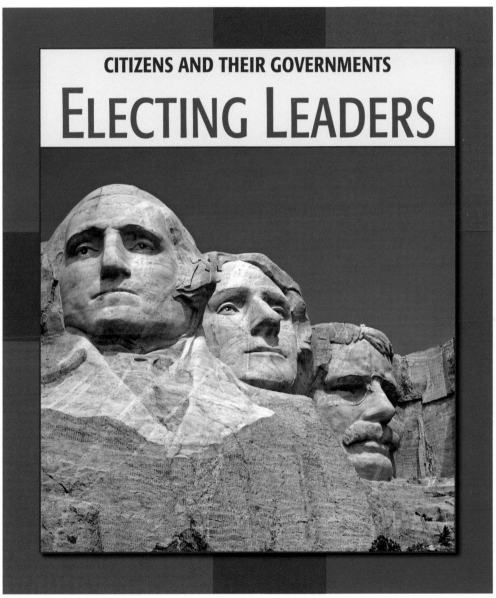

Tamra Orr

Cherry Lake Publishing
Ann Arbor, Michigan

Published in the United States of America by Cherry Lake Publishing
Ann Arbor, MI
www.cherrylakepublishing.com

Photo Credits: Page 4, © Guy Reynolds/Dallas Morning News/CORBIS; Page 6, © Dan Habib/Concord Monitor/CORBIS; Page 7, © Brendan McDermid/epa/CORBIS; Page 10, Photo Courtesy of Library of Congress; Page 13, © Bettmann/CORBIS; Page 14, © McPherson Colin/CORBIS; Page 18, © Joseph Sohm/Visions of America/CORBIS; Page 19, Photo Courtesy of Library of Congress; Page 21, © Comstock/CORBIS; Page 23, © Reuters/CORBIS; Page 25, © Erik Freeland/CORBIS; Page 26, Photo Courtesy of Library of Congress; Page 27, © Owen Franken/CORBIS; Page 29, Photo Courtesy of Library of Congress

Library of Congress Cataloging-in-Publication Data
Orr, Tamra.
 Electing leaders/by Tamra Orr.
    p. cm.—(Citizens and their governments)
  ISBN-13: 978-1-60279-063-6
  ISBN-10: 1-60279-063-9
 1. Elections—United States—Juvenile literature. I. Title. II. Series.
 JK1978.O77 2008
 324.60973—dc22   2007006756

Cherry Lake Publishing would like to acknowledge the work of
The Partnership for 21st Century Skills.
Please visit www.21stcenturyskills.org for more information.

TABLE OF CONTENTS

CHAPTER ONE

CHOOSING LEADERS

*More than 122 million American citizens voted
in the national elections in 2004.*

On Election Day, many Americans from the smallest towns to the largest

cities and everyone in between take the time to vote. Most people trek to

specific polling places to cast their **ballots**. These polling places have set

hours, so voters have to be sure to arrive during the correct time periods.

Bad weather is no excuse!

Sometimes the election is just for local offices. These may be elections for mayors, judges, and city council members. Or they may be for members of the school board or water board. There may even be an election for dogcatcher!

Once every four years in November, however, the election is for president. On those election days, the vote tallies climb, and the whole nation watches TV to get the results of who will be their new city councilman, their new governor, their new state representative—and of course, their new president. It is an exciting time, but it is actually just one part of a long and complex process.

In a democracy, citizens have the right to elect their leaders. However, in recent national elections only about 50 percent of eligible voters cast a vote. Why is it important that people exercise their right to vote? What problems might a small voter turnout cause for elected officials?

Electing a leader, either one for just your community or one for the entire country, is a complicated job. It involves a group of dedicated and determined people, months and months of organizing and planning, and more hard work than most people would imagine. It takes a lot of teamwork from volunteers and professionals alike to make a political campaign a success.

Every political campaign, from president on down, depends on hundreds if not thousands of volunteers.

Voters in California elected Arnold Schwarzenegger governor, seen here taking the oath of office.

Starting Young

Although it may seem to you that all of the leaders running for office

are adults, there are actually some young people who have won political

races, too. David Wichlinski, a senior at Indiana's Boone Grove High

School, was elected to the city's township board. "I know you kids look at

government as something for people with gray hair, but it's important we get involved in it now," he said after taking his oath of office.

Another person who entered politics at a young age is Kyle Andrews. At the age of 21, as a senior at Niagara University in New York, he was elected in 2004 to the county legislature. During the day, he went to classes, ate in the cafeteria, and went to the college's basketball games. In the evening, he turned into Kyle Andrews, Democrat!

CHAPTER TWO

WHAT MAKES A GOOD CANDIDATE?

All people running for office spend as much time as possible meeting with potential voters.

All jobs require a certain set of skills and personality traits. It is very

hard for a shy person to be successful in sales or for someone who is not

good at details to succeed as an accountant. The same is true for political

*The House chamber, as shown in this 1920 photo, has seats for
every member as well as galleries above for visitors.*

candidates. They have to have certain attitudes and abilities if they are

going to succeed in politics. Just who makes a good candidate?

Just How Old Is That?

Local governments usually require that a candidate for office be

at least 18 years old. Requirements for election to the U.S. House of

Representatives and the Senate are more stringent.

Representatives must be:

- at least 25 years old

- a U.S. citizen for at least seven years

- a resident of the state from which he or she

  is elected

Senators must be:

- at least 30 years old

- a U.S. citizen for at least nine years

- a resident of the state from which he or she

  is elected

The requirements for president of the United

States are even stricter. Such candidates must be:

- at least 35 years old

- a natural-born U.S. citizen

- a resident of the U.S. for at least 14 years

What personal traits do you think make a good politician? How do you fit that list? Does politician sound like an interesting profession?

There are many other requirements other than age and where a person lives, however. There are important personality traits that will make one person a better politician than another.

Political candidates must not only be dedicated and have a passion for helping others. They must also be able to keep a positive attitude, even when things go wrong. New York Congressman Emmanuel Celler served in the U.S. House of Representatives for half a century. He once put it this way, "One must have the friendliness of a child, the enthusiasm of a teenager, the assurance of a college boy . . . the curiosity of a cat and the good humor of an idiot."

Political scientists study elections, and many of these scientists say that the best candidates are those who have a powerful combination of several traits. The best candidates have a great deal of heart and commitment. They also have strong organizational skills, a willingness to work hard, endless determination, and finally, a positive attitude. Entering the world of politics is a huge commitment of time, energy, and effort!

Congressman Emmanuel Celler, like Everett Dirkson, Sam Rayburn, Carl Vinson, and others, served in either the U.S. House or Senate for several decades in the 1900s.

CHAPTER THREE

MEET THE CAMPAIGN TEAM

*Like all leaders in democratic nations, Prime Minister Tony Blair
and his large campaign team met frequently with voters.*

When someone runs for office, it is easy to think that he or she stands

alone. However, behind every speech, opinion, and event is a group of

people who are just as dedicated as the candidate. How many people are

on this team depends on the level of office. Clearly, a campaign team for a

city council spot will be much smaller than one for U.S. president!

Each person on the campaign team has an important job. The **campaign manager** oversees the entire process. He or she assigns responsibilities to various campaign workers, sets the final schedules, and makes important decisions on behalf of the candidate. It is the campaign manager's job to create the **campaign plan,** which is an outline of what strategy and tactics the candidate will use to get as many votes as possible. It includes what issues to emphasize, what groups of people to target, and which geographic areas to focus on.

The campaign manager's job is immense, and he or she has many assistants. These helpers are called

21st Century Content

One of the most important skills in civic literacy is being informed. This means understanding the key issues. People can stay informed by reading or listening to news reports from respected sources. Being informed allows citizens to evaluate candidates' media messages, speeches, and campaign promises.

Much of a campaign manager's job involves planning, planning, planning.

consultants, and they are usually experts in different areas. They may be experts in specific issues such as immigration or health to help the candidate work out a policy on the issue. Or they may be consultants with expertise in parts of the campaign process. For example, the media consultant makes sure that radio, TV, and newspaper reporters are invited to all speeches and other events. The media consultant may also develop advertisements for TV, radio, and elsewhere that include the candidate's **slogan.**

A **pollster** conducts surveys to better understand public opinion. Since polls can be expensive, they are most often used by candidates for state or national office.

The campaign **treasurer** deals with the campaign budget, writing checks, and accepting donations. This can be a very difficult job because there are strict laws about how much money can be donated to a campaign by a single person. Other laws require detailed reports of how donations are spent.

Without a doubt, the **volunteers** are among the most important people on the campaign team. They are the ones who willingly put in countless

Why do you think there are laws about who can donate money to a political campaign? Hint: Think about what would happen if one very rich person wanted to influence decisions about a key issue.

hours licking envelopes, answering phones, folding brochures, and doing other necessary but tedious tasks. They put up yard signs, tie brochures to doorknobs, make the office coffee, and work at campaign events. They do this without any payment at all because they are dedicated to the candidate's victory. Without volunteers, most campaigns would fall apart quickly.

These campaign volunteers for Ross Perot prepare mailings
and make phone calls to registered voters.

CHAPTER FOUR

ON THE CAMPAIGN TRAIL

President William H. Taft made a "Whistle Stop" train journey across the country to speak to voters when he ran for president.

The process of preparing for an election usually starts long before the actual day of voting. Potential candidates sometimes spend years thinking about running for office, talking to friends and relatives, and sizing up the competition. Then the election campaign begins with the candidate's announcement that he or she plans to run for office. From that moment,

the race is on! Each one of the days after that is full of activities designed to put the person in office as effectively and efficiently as possible.

Getting the Word Out

Getting a candidate's face, opinions, and personality known to the city, state, or country is a complex job. There are three ways that most candidates do this.

The first one is called the personal aspect. This is where the candidate meets the public and explains his or her political position on issues through endless appearances, press conferences, interviews, and speeches. This calls for good skills in public speaking, as well as diplomacy and great manners.

Campaign buttons have been popular with collectors—and voters—for many decades.

The second part of the campaign is the *organizational aspect*. The team contacts special interest groups, raises money, and gets support or **endorsements** from individuals and organizations. Often this involves giving out many "freebies." These are shirts, buttons, hats, pens, magnets, yard signs, and bumper stickers with the candidate's name on them that

interested voters can get for free. Studies have shown that the more times people see a candidate's name, the more likely they are to vote for that person.

With the media aspect, advertisements for the candidate are run on television and radio and in magazines and newspapers. Some ads are sent through the mail while others use recorded messages that are sent directly to people's telephones. Campaigns may also use billboards along key roads. All of these types of ads are often quite effective. They usually feature the candidate's slogan and remind people to be sure to vote when Election Day rolls around.

*In 2000, presidential candidates Al Gore and George W. Bush held
a debate in Boston that was shown on TV across the nation.*

A key event may be a public **debate** between opposing candidates. This

has been a common event for more than 150 years. One famous series of

debates took place in Illinois between Abraham Lincoln and Stephen A.

Douglas when they were running for the U.S. Senate in the 1850s. Today,

candidates at all levels often debate each other.

Debates on TV between key presidential candidates have become common since 1960. In that year, John Kennedy and Richard Nixon debated each other. Some political scientists say that Kennedy's calm, youthful presence helped him win both the debate and the election because Nixon looked tense and pressured.

On to the Convention!

Once every four years, the two major political parties, the Republicans and the Democrats, hold political **conventions. Delegates** from across the country come together to support the party's chosen presidential candidate. The delegates discuss issues, listen to speeches, and even attend "pep rallies." These conventions were once used to actually select a party's presidential candidate, but all that changed when reporters—especially TV reporters and their cameras—were allowed in. Many politicians did not want the public to see them arguing or, worse, hear a protestor interrupt a speech with jeering or negative opinions.

National conventions are usually big, loud, fun affairs with lots of balloons and confetti.

CHAPTER FIVE

THE PROCESS OF GOVERNING

As President Harry Truman once said, "Politics—good politics—is public service. There is no life or occupation in which a man can find a greater opportunity to serve his community and his country." Most of the people who are elected to office today would agree. Getting elected is just the starting point to actually doing the job.

And what is that job? It depends on the position to which the candidate was elected. For example, the mayor of Milwaukee

President Dwight D. Eisenhower is a good example of "public service." Before becoming president, he spent his career in the Army and led Allied forces in Europe in World War II.

doesn't need to worry about things in Atlanta, Cleveland, or San Jose.

That's up to the mayors in those cities. But a mayor of any city or town

must worry about everything that happens there, even if other people have

been elected to oversee some things.

Usually, anyone elected to office must be prepared to be part of a big

team. Take that mayor for instance. As the head of a local government,

The mayor and city council members in all towns meet regularly with
the public, as is happening here in Asheville, North Carolina.

he or she must work closely with the chief of police, the fire commissioner, and the city council. The same is true for state governments as well as the federal one. The people in those offices must spend the available money wisely. They must successfully address issues that are worrying to voters, such as gangs, unemployment, traffic congestion, property taxes, or a million other things. However, those who are elected to office need to remember that they were elected to serve the people, not the other way around!

People elected to office must also be ready to *lead* in times of crisis. This happened in 1993 when the Mississippi River flooded hundreds of miles of cities and farmland along its borders. President Clinton sent in federal aid to help the people. He even visited the disaster area and talked to suffering people himself to help them get through the crisis.

Whether it is snowstorms, floods, fires, hurricanes, droughts, volcanic eruptions, terrorists, or other disasters, people elected to office are expected to be at the forefront of those who deal with the situation. If they don't do a good job, they can expect to be voted out of office—and soon!

President Franklin Roosevelt was one of America's greatest leaders and steered the nation through the Great Depression and World War II.

GLOSSARY

ballots (BAL-uhts) sheets of paper or cards used to cast votes

campaign manager (kam-PEYN MAN-i-jer) person who oversees a political campaign

campaign plan (kam-PEYN plan) written outline of what the candidate will do during the campaign

consultants (kuhn-SUHL-tnts) experts in a specific area who give advice and provide guidance

conventions (kuhn-VEN-shuhnz) gatherings of delegates to choose candidates

debate (di-BEYT) discussion of issues from opposing viewpoints

delegates (DEL-i-gits) representatives of a group

endorsements (en-DAWRS-muhnts) approval of and support for a political candidate

pollster (POHL-ster) expert who conducts surveys to determine public support for an issue

slogan (SLOH-guhn) brief statement of purpose or motto

treasurer (TREZH-er-er) person who manages finances

volunteers (vol-uhn-TEERZ) people who work on a political campaign or other project for free

FOR MORE INFORMATION

Books

Boyers, Sara Jane. *Teen Power Politics.*
Brookfield, CT: Millbrook Press, 2000.

Donovan, Sandra. *Running for Office: A Look at Political Campaigns.* Minneapolis, MN: Lerner Publishing, 2003.

Dukakis, Michael. *How to Get into Politics—and Why: A Reader.* Wilmington, MA: Great Source Education Group, 2006.

Klee, Sheila. *Volunteering for a Political Campaign.*
New York: Children's Press, 2000.

Kowalski, Kathiann. *Campaign Politics: What's Fair? What's Foul?* Minneapolis, MN: Lerner Publications, 2001.

Magstadt, Thomas. *Understanding Politics: Ideas, Institutions and Issues.* Belmont, CA: Wadsworth/Thompson Learning, 2005.

Perry, Susan. *Catch the Spirit: Teen Volunteers Tell How They Made a Difference.* New York: Franklin Watts, 2000.

Other Media

To find out more about elections in the United States, go to
http://www.congressforkids.net/Elections_index.htm

INDEX

ABOUT THE AUTHOR

Tamra Orr is a full-time writer and author living in the gorgeous Pacific Northwest. She loves her job because she learns more about the world every single day and then turns that information into pop quizzes for her patient and tolerant children (ages 16, 13, and 10). She has written more than 80 nonfiction books for people of all ages, so she never runs out of material and is sure she'd be a champion on *Jeopardy!*